آسف لقد سرقت قطتك

شكرا لإطعامها بينما أنا بعيدا

Marcy Schaaf

Arabic

Sorry I Stole Your Cat

Thanks for Feeding Her While I'm Away

Marcy Schaaf

Meet Delila, the lovable cat whose life takes an unexpected turn when her family gets a new puppy. Feeling left out and overwhelmed, Delila finds a new home next door with a kind single lady. But when the lady goes on vacation, Delila's old family steps in to help, and everyone learns a valuable lesson about change and love.

Sorry I Stole Your Cat, Thanks for Feeding Her While I'm Away is a true story from Pahoa, Hawaii.

This delightful tale shows that even when life changes, it can still be filled with love, happiness, and new beginnings.
Join Delila on her heartwarming adventure and discover that no matter what happens, it's okay to embrace change!

This book is dedicated to Lux and Tula, the amazing kids next door.

Thank you for sharing your wonderful cat, Delila, with such open hearts and allowing her love to fill my life. Your kindness and understanding meant the world to both of us. Delila brought joy and comfort to my home when I needed it the most, and I hope she brought just as much happiness to yours.

Life has a funny way of bringing us together in the most unexpected ways, and I'm so grateful that our paths crossed. Lux and Tula, your generosity and love made all the difference, and for that, I am forever thankful.

Your friend and Neighbor,
Marcy Schaaf

Once there was a cat named Delila.

ذات مرة كان هناك قطة اسمها دليلة.

She lived with a family of four.

عاشت مع عائلة مكونة من أربعة أفراد.

Mom, Dad, a girl, and a boy.

أُمِّي وأَبِي وفتاةٌ وصبِيٌّ.

One day
they got a new puppy.

في أحد الأيام حصلوا على جرو جديد.

The puppy ate Delila's food.

أكل الجرو طعام دليلة.

The puppy chased her around.

طاردها الجرو حولها.

It even took her spot in bed!

حتى أنها أخذت مكانها في السرير!

Delila was old and
didn't wanna play with the puppy.

كانت دليلة كبيرة في السن ولم تكن تريد اللعب مع الجرو.

She found a peaceful
home next door.

وجدت منزلاً هادئًا مجاورًا.

A lady lived there alone.

سيدة تعيش هناك وحدها.

The lady planted catnip for Delila.

زرعت السيدة النعناع البري لدليلا.

She gave Delila lots of love.

لقد أعطت ديليلا الكثير من الحب.

Delila had a new comfy spot.

In the lady's master bedroom.

حصلت ديليلا على مكان مريح جديد.

في غرفة النوم الرئيسية للسيدة.

One day the lady
went on vacation.
TA
TRAVELER

ذات يوم ذهبت السيدة في إجازة.

She asked the kids
next door for help.

طلبت المساعدة من الأطفال المجاورين.

"Sorry I stole your cat," she said.

قالت: "آسفة لأنني سرقت قطتك".

"Thanks for feeding her
while I'm away."

"شكرا لإطعامها
بينما أنا بعيدا."

The kids missed Delila.

غاب الأطفال عن ديليلا.

They were happy to help.

كانوا سعداء بالمساعدة.

They fed Delila every day.

لقد أطعموا دليلة كل يوم.

They played with her, too.

لقد لعبوا معها أيضًا.

Delila felt loved and happy.

شعرت دليلة بالحب والسعادة.

She had the best of both worlds.

كان لديها أفضل ما في العالمين.

A quiet home and playful kids.

منزل هادئ وأطفال مرحين.

When the lady returned,
she thanked them.

وعندما عادت السيدة شكرتهم.

Delila purred contentedly.

She was right where
she should be!

خرخرة دليلة بارتياح.

لقد كانت على حق حيث ينبغي أن تكون!

Life changes sometimes
and that's okay.

الحياة تتغير في بعض الأحيان
وهذا جيد.

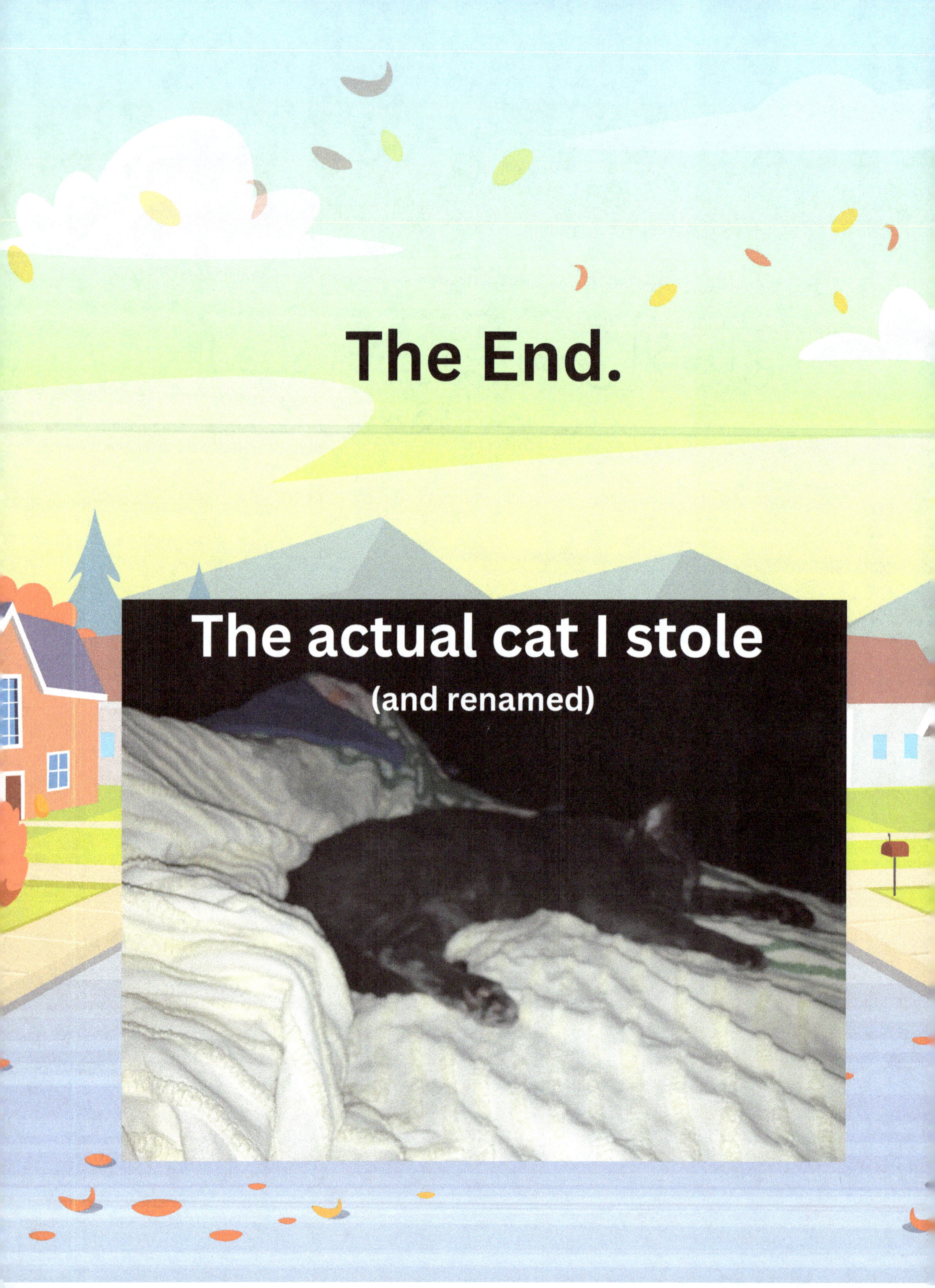

The End.
The actual cat I stole
(and renamed)

The real kids next door

Books By Schaaf

www.BookBySchaaf.com

Find us at: